Masters of Success

The MASTERS
Of Success

Table of Contents

Masters of Success

Chapter One

KEN BLANCHARD

KEN BLANCHARD

THE INTERVIEW

David Wright (Wright)

Few people have created a positive impact on the day-to-day management of people and companies more than Dr. Kenneth Blanchard who is known around the world simply as Ken, a prominent, gregarious, sought after author, speaker, and business consultant. Ken is universally characterized by friends, colleagues, and clients as one of the most insightful, powerful, and compassionate men in the business today.

Ken's impact as a writer is far-reaching. His phenomenal best-selling book, *One Minute Manager*, co-authored with Spencer Johnson, has sold more than nine million copies worldwide and has been translated into more than twenty-five languages. Ken is Chairman and "Chief Spiritual Officer" of the Ken Blanchard Companies. The organization's focus is to energize organizations around the world with customized training in bottom line business strategies that are based on the simple yet powerful principles inspired by Ken's best-selling books.

Dr. Blanchard, welcome to *Masters of Success*!

Dr. Ken Blanchard (Blanchard)

Well, it's nice to talk to you, David. It's good to be here.

Wright

I must tell you that preparing for your interview took quite a bit more time than usual. The scope of your life's work and your business, the Ken Blanchard Companies, would make for a dozen fascinating interviews. Before we dive into the specifics of some of your projects and strategies, will you give our readers a brief synopsis of your life, how you came to be the Ken Blanchard that we all know and respect?

Blanchard

Well, I'll tell you, David, I think life is what happens when you are planning on doing something else. I forget whose line that was; but I never intended to do what I have been doing. In fact, all my professors in college told me I couldn't write. I wanted to do college work, which I did. They told me, "You had better be an administrator." So I decided I was going to be a Dean of Men, a Dean of Students. I got provisionally accepted into my master's degree program, and then provisionally accepted at Cornell, because I never could take any of those standardized tests.

I took the College Boards four times and finally got 502 in English. My mind doesn't work. I ended up in a higher university in Athens, Ohio, in 1966 as Administrative Assistant to the Dean of the Business School. When I got there, he said, "Ken, I want you to teach a course. I want all my deans to teach." I had never thought about teaching because they said I couldn't write and you had to publish.

He put me in the manager's department. I've taken enough bad courses in my day; I wasn't going to teach one. So I really prepared and had a wonderful time with the students. I was chosen as one of the top ten teachers on the campus coming out of the chute. I just had a marvelous time. A colleague by the name of Paul Hershey was chairman of the management department, and he wasn't real friendly to me initially because the Dean had led me into his department. But I heard he was a great teacher. He taught organizational behavior and leadership. So I asked him if I could sit in on his course next semester.

"Nobody audits my courses," he replied. "If you want to take it for credit, you're welcome." I couldn't believe it. I had a doctorate degree and he wanted me to take his course for credit. So I signed up. The registrar didn't know what to do with me because I already had a doctorate, but I wrote the papers and took the course, and it was great.

In June 1967, Hershey came into my office and said, "Ken, I've been teaching in this field for ten years. I think I'm better than anybody, but I can't write. I'm a nervous wreck, and I'd love to write a textbook with somebody. Would you write one with me?"

I said, "We ought to be a great team. You can't write and I'm not supposed to, so let's do it!" So thus began this great career of writing and teaching. We wrote a textbook called, *Management of Organizational Behavior Utilizing Human Resources*. It just came out with its eighth edition last year and it sold more than any other textbook in its field throughout the years. It's been more than thirty-five years since that book came out.

I quit my administrative job, became a professor, and I worked my way up through the ranks. I took a sabbatical leave and went to California for one year twenty-five years ago. I met Spencer Johnson at a cocktail party. Spencer wrote children's books; he has a wonderful series called, *Value Tales for Kids: The Value of Courage, The Story of Jackie Robinson; The Value of Believing In Yourself, The Story Louis Pasteur*. My wife, Margie, met him first and told me, "You guys ought to write a book together—a children's book for managers, because they won't read anything else." That was my introduction to Spencer. So, our book, the *One Minute Manager* was really a kid's book for big people. That is a long way from saying my career was well planned.

Wright

Ken, what and/or who were your early influences in the areas of business, leadership, and success? In other words, who shaped you in your early years?

Blanchard

My father had a great impact on me. He was retired as an Admiral in the Navy and had a wonderful philosophy. I remember when I was elected to president of the seventh grade, and I came home all pumped up. My father said, "Son, it's great that you're the president of the seventh grade, but now that you have that leadership position, don't ever use it." He said, "Great leaders are followed because people respect them and like them, not because they have power." That was a wonderful lesson for me early on. He was just a great model for me. I got a lot from him.

Then I had this wonderful opportunity in the mid 1980s to write a book with Norman Vincent Peale, author of, *The Power of Positive Thinking*. I met him when he was eighty-six years old. We were asked to write a book on ethics together and we wrote, *The Power of Ethical Management: Integrity Pays, You Don't Have to Cheat to Win*. It didn't matter what we were writing together, I learned so much from him; he just added to what I learned from my mother. When I was born my mother said, "I laughed before I cried, I danced before I walked, and I smiled before I frowned." So that, on top of Norman Vincent Peale, really made me I focus on what I could do to train leaders. I asked questions like: How do you make them positive? How do you make them realize that it's not about them—it's about whom they are serving? It's not about their position—it's about what they can do to help other people win. So, I'd say my mother and father, and then Norman Vincent Peale had a tremendous impact on me.

Wright

I can imagine. I read a summery of your undergraduate and graduate degrees. I assumed you studied business administration, marketing management, and related courses. Instead, at Cornell, you studied government and philosophy. You received your master's from Colgate in sociology and counseling and your Ph.D. from Cornell in educational administration and leadership. Why did you choose this course of study? How has it affected your writing and consulting?

Blanchard

Well, again, it wasn't really well planned out. I originally went to Colgate to get a master's degree in education, because I was going to be a Dean of Students over men. I had been a government major, and I was a government major because it was the best department in Cornell in the Liberal Arts School. It was exciting. We would study what the people were doing at the league governments.

The Philosophy Department was also great. I just loved the philosophical arguments. I wasn't a great student in terms of grades, but I'm a total learner. I would sit there and listen and I would really soak it in. When I went over to Colgate and got involved in the education courses, they were awful—they were boring. By the second week, I was sitting at the bar at the Colgate Inn saying, "I can't believe I've been here two years for this."

This is just the way the Lord works: sitting next to me in the bar is a young sociology professor who had just got his Ph.D. at Illinois, and his wife was back packing up. He was staying at the Inn and I was moaning and groaning about what I was doing. He said to me, "Why don't you come and major with me in sociology? It's really exciting."

"I can do that?" I asked.

He said, "Yes."

I knew they would probably let me do whatever I wanted the first week. Suddenly, I switched out of education and went with Warren Ramshaw. He had a tremendous impact on me. He retired a few years ago as the leading professor at Colgate in the Arts and Sciences, and got me interested in leadership and organizations. That's why I got a master's in sociology.

Then the reason I went into educational administration and leadership was because it was a doctoral program I could get into. The reason for that was I knew the guy heading up the program. He said, "The greatest thing about Cornell is that you will be in a School of Education. It's not very big, so you don't have to take many education courses, and you can take stuff all over the place." That was a marvelous man by the name of Don McCarty, who ended up going on to be the Dean of the School of Education, Wisconsin. He had an impact on my life, but I was always searching around.

My mission statement is, "To be a loving teacher and example of simple truths that help myself and others to awaken to the presence of God in our lives." The reason I mention "God" is, I believe the biggest addiction in the world is the human ego. I'm really into simple truth, however. I used to tell people I was trying to get the B.S. out of the behavioral sciences.

Wright

I can't help but think, when you mentioned your father, that he just bottomed-lined it for you about leadership.

Blanchard

Yes.

Wright

Years ago when I went to a conference in Texas, a man named Paul Myers said, "David, if you think you're a leader and you look around and no one is following you, you're just out for a walk."

Blanchard

Well, you'd get a kick out of this: I'm just reaching over to pick up a picture of Paul Myers on my desk; he's a good friend. We co-founded the Center for Faith Walk Leadership here where we're trying to challenge and equip people to lead like Jesus. It's non-profit, and I tell people I'm not an evangelist because we've got enough trouble with the Christians we have—we don't need any more new ones. But, this is a picture of Paul on top of a mountain, and then another picture below of him under the sea with stingrays. It says, "Attitude is everything. Whether you're on the top of the mountain or the bottom of the sea, true happiness is achieved by accepting God's promises, and by having a biblically positive frame of mind. Your attitude is everything." Isn't that something?

Wright

He's a fine, fine man. He helped me tremendously. In keeping with the theme of our book, *Conversations On Success,* I wanted to get a sense from you about your own success journey. Many people know you best from the *One Minute Manager* books you coauthored with Spencer Johnson. Would you consider these books as a high water mark for you, or have you defined success for yourself in different terms?

Blanchard

Well, you know the *One Minute Manager* was an absurdly success-ful book. It achieved success so quickly I found I couldn't take credit for it. So that was when I really got on my own spiritual journey and started to try to find out what the real meaning of life and success was. That's been a wonderful journey for me because I think, David, the problem with most people is they think their self-worth is a func-tion of their performance plus the opinion of others. The minute you define your self-worth like that, every day your self-worth is up for grabs because your performance is going to fluctuate on a day-to-day basis. People are fickle—their opinions are going to go up and down. So, you need to ground your self-worth in the unconditional love God has ready for us.

That concept grew out of the unbelievable success of the *One Min-ute Manager.* When I started to realize where all that came from, that's how I got involved in the ministry I mentioned. Paul Myers is a part of it. As I started to read the Bible, I realized that everything I've ever written about, or taught, Jesus did. You know, He did it with twelve incompetent guys He hired. The only guy with much education was Judus, who was His only turnover problem.

Wright

Right.

Blanchard

So it was a really interesting thing. What I see in people is not only do they think their self-worth is a function of their performance plus the opinion of others, but they measure their success on the amount of accumulation of wealth, on recognition, power, and status. I think those are nice success items—there's nothing wrong with those, as long as you don't define your life by them.

What I think is a better focus rather than success is what Bob Buford, in his book *Half Times,* calls "significance"—move from success to significance.

I think the opposite of accumulation of wealth is generosity. I wrote a book called, *The Generosity Factor* with Truett Cathy, founder of Chick-fil-A. He is one of the most generous men I've ever met in my life. I thought we needed to have a model of generosity—generosity not only with your treasure, but also your time and talent. Truett and I added *touch* as a fourth one.

The opposite of recognition is service. I think you become an adult when you realize you're here to serve rather than to be served.

Finally, the opposite of power and status is having loving relationships. Mother Theresa is a good example. She couldn't have cared less about recognition, power, and status because she was focused on generosity, service, and loving relationships. She did get all of that earthly stuff such as recognition and status; but if you focus on the earthly, such as money, recognition, and power, you're never going to get to significance. I you focus on significance, you'll be amazed at how much success can come your way.

Wright

I spoke with Truett Cathy recently and was impressed by what a down-to-earth good man he seems to be. He has Chick-fil-A close on Sundays. When my friends found out I had talked to him, they said, "Boy, he must be a great Christian man, but he's rich." I told them, "Well, to put his faith into perspective, closing on Sunday costs him $500 million a year." He lives his faith, doesn't he?

Blanchard

Absolutely, but he still outsells everybody else.

Wright

That's right.

Blanchard

They were recently chosen the number one fast quick service restaurant in Los Angeles. They only have five restaurants here and they've only been here for a year.

Wright

The simplest market scheme, I told him, tripped me up. I walked by the first Chick-fil-A I had ever seen, and some girl came out with chicken stuck on toothpicks and handed me one. I just grabbed it and ate it and it's history from there on.

Blanchard

Yes, I think so. It's really special. It is so important that people understand generosity, service, and loving relationships because too many people are running around like a bunch of peacocks. You even see pastors who ask, "How many in your congregation are authors, how many books have you sold?" or, regarding business, "What's your profit margin? What's your sales?" The reality is, that's all well and good, but I think what you need to focus on is others. I think if businesses did that more and we got Wall Street off our backs with all the short-term evaluation, we'd be a lot better off.

Wright

Absolutely. There seems to be a clear theme that winds through many of your books that have to do with success in business and organizations and that is how management treats people and how they feel about their value to a company. Is this an accurate observation? If so, can you elaborate on it?

Blanchard

Yes, it's a very accurate observation. See, I think "profit" is the applause you get for taking care of your customers and creating a motivating environment for your people. Very often people believe business is only about the bottom line. But no, the bottom line happens to be the result of creating customers who are raving fans. I described this with Sheldon Bowles in our book. Customers want to brag about you, and then create an environment where people can be gung-ho and committed. You've got to take care of your customers and your people, and then your cash register is going to go ka-ching. Then is when you can make some big bucks.

Wright

I noticed that your professional title with the Ken Blanchard Companies is somewhat unique, Chairman and "Chief Spiritual Officer." What does your title mean to you personally and to your company? How does it affect the books you choose to write?

Blanchard

I remember having lunch with Max DuPree one time. He's the legendary Chairman of Herman Miller, Inc. He wrote a wonderful book called, *Leadership is an Art*. I asked him, "What's your job?"

He said, "I basically work in the vision area."

"Well, what do you do?" I asked.

"I'm like a third grade teacher," He said, "I say our vision and values over, and over, and over again until people get it right, right, right."

I decided then I was going to become our Chief Spiritual Officer. I would be working in the vision, values, and energy part of our business. We have about 275 to 300 around the country, in Canada, and the U.K., and we have partners in about thirty nations. I leave a voice mail every morning for everybody in the company, and I do three things regarding that as Chief Spiritual Officer:

1. People tell me what we need to pray for,
2. People tell me about those we need to praise—our unsung heroes and people like that and,
3. I leave an inspirational morning message every day.

I am really the cheerleader—the "energy bunny"—in our company, and the one who reminds us why we're here and what we're trying to do. Our business in the Ken Blanchard Companies is to help people to lead at a higher level, and to help individuals, and organizations. Our mission statement is, "To unleash the power and potential of people and organizations for the common good." So if we are going to do that, we've really got to believe in that. I'm working on getting more Chief Spiritual Officers around the country. I think it's a great title—we should get more of them.

Wright

So those people for whom you pray, where do you get the names?

Blanchard

The people in the company tell me who needs help, whether it's a spouse who is sick, or kids who are sick, or they are worried about something. We've got more than five years of data about the power of prayer, which is pretty important.

For example, this morning my inspirational message was about my wife and five members of our company who walked sixty miles last weekend—twenty miles a day for three days—to raise money for breast cancer research. It was amazing. I went down and waved them all in as they came. There was a ceremony where it was announced they had raised 7.6 million dollars. There were more than three thousand people walking—and a lot of the walkers were dressed in pink—who were cancer victors, people who had overcome cancer. There were even men who were walking with pictures of their wives who had died from breast cancer. I thought it was incredible.

There wasn't one mention of it in the major San Diego papers on Monday. I said, "Isn't that just something." I said, "We have to be an island of positive influence because you know all you see in the paper today is about Michael Jackson and Scott Peterson and Coby Bryant and this kind of thing, when here you have all these thousands of people out there walking and trying to make a difference, and nobody thinks it's news." So every morning I pump people up about what life's about and about what's going on. That's what my Chief Spiritual Officer is about.

Wright

I had the pleasure of reading one of your current releases, *The Leadership Pill.*

Blanchard

Yes.

Wright

I must admit that my first thought was how short the book was. I wondered if I was going to get my money's worth, which, by the way, I most certainly did. Many of your books are brief and based on a fictitious story. Most business books in the market today are hundreds of pages in length and read almost like a textbook. Can you talk a little bit about why you write these short books and about the premise of *The Leadership Pill?*

Blanchard

I really got that during my relationship with Spencer Johnson when we wrote the *One Minute Manager.* As you know he wrote *Who Moved My Cheese,* which was a phenomenal success. He wrote children's books, and I was a storyteller. As I said earlier, my wife told me, "You guys ought to write a children's book for managers. They won't read anything else."

Jesus talked by parable. My favorite books were, *Jonathan Livingstone Seagull, The Littlest Prince,* and *Og Mandino,* the greatest of them all. These are all great parables. I started writing parables because people can get into the story and learn the contents of the story without bringing their judgmental hats into their reading. You write a regular book and they'll say, "Well, where did you get the research?" They get into that judgmental side. Our books get them emotionally involved and they learn.

The Leadership Pill is a fun story about a pharmaceutical company convinced they have discovered the secret to leadership and they can put the ingredients in a pill. When they announce it, the country goes crazy because everybody knows we need more effective leaders. When they release it, it outsells Viagra and all those big gray trucks. The founders of the company start selling off stock and they call them Pillionaires.

Then along comes this guy who calls himself "the effective manager," and he challenges them to a no-pill challenge. If they identify two non-performing groups, he'll take on one and let somebody on the pill take another one, and he guarantees his group will out-perform the other group by the end of the year. They agree, but of course, they give him a drug test every week to make sure he's not sneaking pills on the side.

I wrote the book with Marc Muchnick who was a young guy in his early thirties. We did a major study together of what does this interesting "Y" generation—the young people of today—want from leaders, and this is a secret blend that this effective manager in the book uses. When you think about it, David, this is really powerful in terms of what people want from a leader. Number one, they want integrity. Many people have talked about that in the past, but these young people will walk if they see people say one thing and do another. A lot of us walk into the bathroom and out into the halls to talk about it. But these people will quit. They don't want somebody to say something and not do it.

The second thing they want is a partnership relationship. They hate superior/subordinate. I mean, what awful terms those are. It's a case of the head of the department versus the hired hands. Someone asks, "What do you do?" The reply is, "I'm in supervision—I see things a lot clearer than these stupid idiots." They want to be treated as partners. If they can get a financial partnership, that's great. I if they can't, they really want at least a psychological partnership where they can bring their brains to work and make decisions.

Then finally, they want affirmation. They not only want to be caught doing things right, but they want to be affirmed for who they are. They want to be known as a person, not as a number.

So those are the three ingredients this effective manager in the story uses. They are wonderful values if you think of them. Rank order values for any organization is number one: integrity. In our company we call it "ethics"—our number one value. Number two value is partnership. Partnership in our companies is relationships. Number three is affirmation—being affirmed as a human being. I think that ties into relationships, too. They are wonderful values that can drive behavior in a great way.

Wright

I believe most people in today's business culture would agree that success in business has everything to do with successful leadership. In *The Leadership Pill*, you present a simple but profound premise that being in leadership is not something you do *to* people; it's something you do *with* them. At face value, that seems incredibly obvious, but you must have found in your research and in your observations that leaders in today's culture do not get this. Would you speak to that issue?

Blanchard

Yes. I think what often happens is this is the human ego, you know. There are too many leaders out there who are self-serving. They're not serving leaders. They think the sheep are there for the benefit of the shepherd. All the power, money, and famous recognition all reside at the top of the hierarchy. They forget that the real action in business is not at the top, it's in the one-to-one, moment-to-moment interactions your front line people have with your customers, it's how the phone was answered, how problems are dealt with, and those kinds of things. If you don't think you're doing leadership *with* them, rather than *to* them, after a while they won't take care of your customers.

I was at a store recently, it's not Nordstrom's, where I normally would go, and I thought of something I had to share with my wife, Margie. I asked the guy behind the counter in the Men's Wear Department, "Can I use your phone?"

He said, "No," rather emphatically.

I said, "You're kidding me. I can always use the phone at Nordstrom's."

He said, "Look, buddy, they won't let *me* use the phone here, why should I let *you* use the phone?"

That is an example of leadership that's done to them not with them. People want a partnership. People want to be involved in a way that really makes a difference.

Wright

Dr. Blanchard, the time has flown by and there are so many more questions I'd like to ask you. In conclusion, would you mind sharing with our readers some closing thoughts on success? If you were mentoring a small group of men and women, and one of their central goals was to become successful, what kind of advice would you give them?

Blanchard

I would first of all ask, "What are you focused on?" As I said earlier, I think if you are focused on success as being accumulation of money, recognition, power, or status, I think you've got the wrong target.

What you need to really be focused on is how can you be generous in the use of your time, your talent, your treasure, and touch. How can you serve people rather than be served? How can you develop caring, loving relationships with people? My sense is if you will focus on those things, success in the traditional sense will come to you. But if you go out and say, "Man, I'm going to make a fortune, and I'm going to do this," whatever it may be and if you focus on those kinds of things, you might even get some of those numbers. You become an adult, however, when you realize you are here to give rather than to get. You're here to serve not to be served. I would just say to people, "Life is such a very special occasion. Don't miss it by aiming at a target that bypasses other people, because we're really here to serve each other." That's what I would share with people.

Wright

Well, what an enlightening conversation, Dr. Blanchard. I really want you to know how much I appreciate all the time you've taken with me for this interview. I know that our readers will learn from this, and I really appreciate your being with us today.

Blanchard

Well, thank you so much, David. I really enjoyed my time with you. You've asked some great questions that made me think. I hope my answers are helpful to other people because, as I say, life is a special occasion.

Wright

Today we have been talking with Dr. Ken Blanchard. He is author of the phenomenal best selling book, *The One Minute Manager*. The fact that he's the "Chief Spiritual Officer" of his company should give us all cause to think about how we are leading our companies and leading our families and leading anything whether it is within church or civic organizations. I know I will.

Thank you so much, Dr. Blanchard, for being with us today on *Masters of Success*.

Blanchard

Good to be with you, David.

About Dr. Ken Blanchard

Few people have created more of a positive impact on the day-to-day management of people and companies than Dr. Kenneth Blanchard, who is known around the world simply as "Ken." When Ken speaks, he speaks from the heart with warmth and humor. His unique gift is to speak to an audience and communicate with each individual as if they were alone and talking one-on-one. He is a polished storyteller with a knack for making the seemingly complex easy to understand. Ken has been a guest on a number of national television programs, including *Good Morning America and The Today Show*, and has been featured in *Time, People, U.S. News & World Report*, and a host of other popular publications. He earned his bachelor's degree in government and philosophy from Cornell University, his master's degree in sociology and counseling from Colgate University, and his Ph.D. in educational administration and leadership from Cornell University.

Dr. Ken Blanchard
The Ken Blanchard Companies
125 State Place
Escondido, California 92029
Phone: 800.728.6000
Fax: 760.489.8407
www.blanchardtraining.com

Chapter Two

JACK CANFIELD

JACK CANFIELD

THE INTERVIEW

David E. Wright (Wright)

Today we are talking with Jack Canfield. You probably know him as the founder and co-creator of the *New York Times* number one best-selling *Chicken Soup for the Soul* book series, which currently has thirty-five titles and seventy-eight million copies in print in over thirty-two languages. Jack's background includes a Batchelor's from Harvard, a Master's from the University of Massachusetts and an Honorary Doctorate from the University of Santa Monica. He has been a high school and university teacher, a workshop facilitator, a psychotherapist, and for the past twenty-five years, a leading authority in the area of self-esteem and personal development.

Jack Canfield, welcome to *Masters of Success!*

Jack Canfield (Canfield)

Thank you David. It's great to be with you.

Wright

I talked with Mark Victor Hansen a few days ago. He gave you full credit for coming up with the idea of the *Chicken Soup* series. Obviously it's made you an internationally known personality. Other than recognition, has the series changed you personally and if so, how?

Canfield

I would say that it has and I think in a couple of ways. Number one, I read stories all day long of people who've overcome what would feel like insurmountable obstacles. For example we just did a book *Chicken Soup for the Unsinkable Soul*. There's a story in there about a single mother with three daughters. She got a disease and she had to have both of her hands and both of her feet amputated. She got prosthetic devices and was able to learn how to use them so she could cook, drive the car, brush her daughters' hair, get a job, etc. I read that and I think, "God, what would I ever have to complain and whine and moan about?" So I think at one level it's just given me a great sense of gratitude and appreciation for everything I have and made me less irritable about the little things.

I think the other thing that's happened for me personally is my sphere of influence has changed. By that I mean, for example, a couple of years ago I was asked to be the keynote speaker for the Women's Congressional Caucus. The Congressional Caucus includes women in Congress, Senators, Governors, and Lieutenant Governors in America.

I asked, "What do you want me to talk about—what topic?"

"Whatever you think we need to know to be better legislators," was the reply.

And I thought, "Wow! They want *me* to tell *them* about what laws they should be making and what would make a better culture?"

Well, that wouldn't have happened if our books hadn't come out and I hadn't become famous. I think I get to play with people at a higher level and have more influence in the world. That's important to me because my life purpose is inspiring and empowering people to live their highest vision so the world works for everybody. I get to do that on a much bigger level than when I was just a high school teacher back in Chicago.

Wright

I think one of the powerful components of that book series is that you can read a positive story in just a few minutes. You can also come back and revisit it. I know my daughter who is thirteen now has three of the books and she just reads them interchangeably. Sometimes I go in her bedroom and she'll be crying and reading one of them. Other times she'll be laughing, so they really are chicken soup for the soul, aren't they?

Canfield

They really are. In fact we have four books in the *Teenage Soul* series now and a new one coming out at the end of this year. We have a new book called *Chicken Soup for the Teenage Soul and the Tough Stuff*. It's all about dealing with parents' divorces, teachers who don't understand you, boyfriends who drink and drive, and stuff like that.

I have a son who's eleven and he has twelve-year-old friend (a girl). I asked my son's friend, "Why do you like this book?"

She said, "You know, whenever I'm feeling down I read it; it makes me cry and I feel better. Some of the stories make me laugh and some of the stories make me feel more responsible for my life. But basically I just feel like I'm not alone."

One of the people I work with recently said that the books are like a support group between the covers of a book. People can read about others' experiences and realize they're not the only one going through something.

Wright

Jack, with our *Masters of Success* publication we're trying to encourage people in our audience to be better, to live better, and be more fulfilled by listening to the examples of our guests. Is there anything or anyone in your life who has made a difference for you and helped you to become a better person?

Canfield

Yes and we could do ten shows just on that. I'm influenced by people all the time. If I were to go way back I'd have to say one of the key influences in my life was Jesse Jackson when he was still a minister in Chicago. I was teaching in an all black high school there and I went to Jesse Jackson's church with a friend one time. What happened for me was I saw somebody with a vision. (This was before Martin Luther King was killed and Jesse was of the lieutenants in his organization.) I just saw people trying to make the world work better for a certain segment of the population. I was inspired by that kind of visionary belief that it's possible to make change.

Then later John F. Kennedy was a hero of mine. I was very much inspired by him.

Later, a therapist by the name of Robert Resnick that I had for two years was an inspiration for me. He taught me a little formula called $E + R = O$. That stands for Events plus Response equals Outcome. He said, "If you don't like your outcomes quit blaming the events and start changing your responses." One of his favorite phrases was, "If the grass on the other side of the fence looks greener, start watering your own lawn more."

I think it helped me get off of any kind of self-pity I might have had because I had parents who were alcoholics. It's very easy to blame them for my life not working. They weren't real successful or rich and I was surrounded by people who were. I felt like, "God, what if I'd had parents like they had? I could have been a lot better." He just got me off that whole notion and made me realize the hand you were dealt is the hand you've got to play and take responsibility for who you are and quit complaining and blaming others and get on with your life. That was a turning point for me.

I'd say the last person who really affected me big time was a guy named W. Clement Stone who was a self-made multi-millionaire in Chicago. He taught me that success is not a four-letter word, it's nothing to be ashamed of and you ought to go for it. He said, "The best thing you can do for the poor is not be one of them." Be a model for what it is to live a successful life. So I learned from him the principles of success and that's what I've been teaching now for the last almost thirty years.

Wright

He was the entrepreneur in the insurance industry, wasn't he?

Canfield

He was. He had combined insurance and when I worked for him he was worth six hundred million dollars. That was before the dot.com millionaires came along in Silicon Valley. He just knew more about success. He was a good friend of Napoleon Hill who wrote *Think and Grow Rich*. He was a fabulous mentor. I really learned a lot from him.

Wright

I miss some of the men I listened to when I was a young salesman coming up and he was one of them. Napoleon Hill was another one and Dr. Peale—all of their writings made me who I am today. I'm glad that I got that opportunity.

Canfield

One speaker whose name you probably will remember, Charlie "Tremendous" Jones, says, "Who we are is a result of the books we read and the people we hang out with." I think that's so true and that's why I tell people, "If you want to have high self-esteem hang out with people with high self-esteem. If you want to be more spiritual hang out with spiritual people." We're always telling our children, "Don't hang out with those kids." The reason we don't want them to associate with certain kinds of people is we know how influential people are with each other. I think we need to give ourselves the same advice. Who are we hanging out with? We can hang out with them in books, cassette tapes, CDs, radio shows like yours, and in person.

Wright

One of my favorites was a fellow named Bill Gove from Florida. I talked with him about three or four years ago; he's retired now. His mind is still as quick as it ever was. I thought he was one of the greatest speakers I had ever heard.

What do you think makes up a great mentor? In other words, are there characteristics that mentors seem to have in common?

Canfield

I think there are two obvious ones. One, I think they have to have the time to do it and two, the willingness to do it. And then three, I think they need to be someone who is doing something you want to do.

W. Clement Stone used to tell me, "If you want to be rich hang out with rich people. Watch what they do, eat what they eat, dress the way they dress. Try it on." He wasn't suggesting that I give up my authentic self, but he was pointing out that they probably have habits I didn't have. His advice was to study them—study the people who are already like you. I always ask salespeople in an organization, "Who are the top two or three in your organization?" I tell them to start taking them out to lunch and dinner and for a drink and finding out what they do. Ask them, "What's your secret?" Nine times out of ten they'll be willing to tell you.

It goes back to what we said earlier about asking. I'll go into corporations and I'll say, "Who are the top ten people?"

They'll all tell me and I'll say, "Did you ever ask them what they do that is different than what you do?"

They reply, "No."

"Why not?"

"Well they might not want to tell me."

"How do you know? Did you ever ask them? All they can do is say no. You'll be no worse off than you are now."

So I think with mentors you just look at people who seem to be living the life you want to live and achieving the results you want to achieve. And then what we tell them in our book is, when you approach a mentor they're probably busy and successful and so they haven't got a lot of time. Just ask, "Can I talk to you for ten minutes every month?" If I know it's only going to be ten minutes I'll probably say yes. The neat thing is if I like you I'll always give you more than ten minutes, but that ten minutes gets me in the door.

Wright

In the future are there any more Jack Canfield books authored singularly?

Canfield

Yes, I'm working on two books right now. One's called $E + R = O$ which is that little formula I told you about earlier. I just feel I want to get that out there because every time I give a speech and talk about that the whole room gets so quiet you can hear a pin drop. I can tell that people are really getting value.

Then I'm going to do a series of books on the principles of success. I've got about 150 of them that I've identified over the years. I have a book down the road I want to do that's called *No More Put-Downs* which is a book probably aimed mostly at parents, teachers, and managers. There's a culture we have now of put-down humor whether it's *Married With Children* or *All in the Family*—there's that characteristic of macho put-down humor. There's research now that's showing how bad it is for kids' self-esteem, and for co-workers and for athletes (when the coaches do it) so I want to get that message out there as well.

Wright

It's really not that funny, is it?

Canfield

No. We'll laugh it off because we don't want to look like we're a wimp but underneath we're hurt. The research now shows that you're better off breaking a child's bones than you are breaking their spirit. A bone will heal much more quickly than their emotional spirit will.

Wright

I remember recently reading a survey where people listed the top five people who had influenced them in their lives. I've tried it on a couple of groups at church and other places. In my case (and in the survey that's running) I found that about three out of people's top five mentors are always teachers. I wonder if that's going to be the same in the next decade.

Canfield

I think probably because as children we're in our most formative years. We actually spend more time with our teachers than we do with our parents. Research shows that the average parent only interacts verbally with each of their children only about eight and a half minutes a day. Yet at school you're interacting with your teacher for anywhere from six to eight hours, depending on how long the school day is. This includes interaction with coaches, chorus directors, etc.

I think that in almost everybody's life there's been that one teacher who loved them as a human being, not just as a student—some person they were supposed to fill full of history and English. And that person believed in them and inspired them.

Les Brown is one of the great motivational speakers in the world. If it hadn't been for one teacher who said, "I think you can do more than be in a special ed. class; I think you're the one," he'd probably still be cutting grass in the median strip of the highways in Florida instead of a successful presenter who can receive $35,000 as a keynote speaker.

Wright

I had a conversation one time with Les when he was talking about this wonderful teacher who discovered he was dyslexic. Everybody else called him dumb but this one lady took him under her wing and had him tested. His entire life changed because of her interest in him.

Canfield

I'm on the board of advisors of the Dyslexic Awareness Resource Center here in Santa Barbara. The reason is because I taught at a high school with a lot of kids who were considered "at-risk." They were kids who would end up in gangs and so forth.

What we found over and over was that about seventy-eight percent of all the kids in the juvenile detention centers in Chicago were kids who had learning disabilities—primarily dyslexia—but there were others as well. They were never diagnosed and they weren't doing well in school so they'd drop out. As soon as you drop out of school you become subject to the influence of gangs and other kinds of criminal and drug linked activities.

If these kids had just been diagnosed earlier, we'd have probably gotten rid of half of the juvenile crime in America because there are a lot of really good programs that can teach dyslexics to read and so forth.

Wright

My wife is a teacher and she brings home stories that are heartbreaking about parents not being as concerned about their children as they used to be or not as helpful as they used to be. Did you find that to be a problem when you were teaching?

Canfield

It depends on what kind of district you're in. If it's a poor district the parents could be drugged out, on alcohol, and basically just not available. If you're in a really high rent district the parents are not available because they're both working and coming home tired, or they're jet-setters, or they're working late at the office because they're workaholics. Sometimes it really takes two paychecks to pay the rent anymore. I find that the majority of parents care but often they don't know what to do. They don't know how to discipline their children. They don't know how to help them with their homework. They're not passing on skills that they never got. Unfortunately the trend tends to be like a chain letter. The people with the least amount of skills tend to have the most number of children. The other thing is you get crack babies. In Los Angeles one out of every ten babies born is a crack baby.

Wright

That's unbelievable.

Canfield

Yes and another statistic shows that by the time they're twelve years old, fifty percent of the kids in the U.S. have started experimenting with alcohol. I see a lot of that in the Bible belt. You don't see the big city, urban designer drugs; but there is a lot of alcoholism. Another thing you get, unfortunately, is a lot of familial violence—a lot of kids getting beat up and hit, parents who drink and then explode; as we talked about earlier, child abuse and sexual abuse—you see a lot of that.

Wright

Most people are fascinated by these television shows about being a survivor. What has been the greatest comeback that you have made from adversity in your career or in your life?

Canfield

You know it's funny, I don't think I've had a lot of major failures and setbacks where I had to start over. My life's been kind of on an intentional curve. But I do have a lot of challenges. Mark and I are always setting goals that challenge us. We always say, "The purpose of setting a really big goal is not so that you can achieve it so much, but it's who you become in the process of achieving it."

A friend of mine, Jim Rose, says, "You want to set goals big enough so that in the process of achieving them you become someone worth being."

I think that to be a millionaire is nice but so what? People make the money and then they lose it. People get the big houses and they burn down or Silicon Valley goes belly up and all of a sudden they don't have a big house anymore. But who you became in the process of learning how to do that can never be taken away from you.

What we do is we constantly put big challenges in front of us. Right now we have a book coming out in a month called *Chicken Soup for the Teacher's Soul*. You'll have to make sure to get a copy for your wife. I was a teacher and I was a teacher trainer for years. But in the last seven years, because of the success of the *Chicken Soup* books, I haven't been in the education world that much. I've got to go out and relearn how I market to that world.

I met with a Superintendent of Schools. I met with a guy named Jason Dorsey who's one of the number one consultants in the world in that area. I found out who has the best-selling book in that area. I sat down with his wife for a day and talked about her marketing approaches.

So I believe that if you face any kind of adversity, whether it's you lose your job, your husband dies, you get divorced, you're in an accident like Christopher Reeves and you become paralyzed, or whatever, you simply do what you have to do. You find people who have already handled this and how they did it. You find out either from their books, or from their tapes, or by talking to them, or interviewing them, and you get the support you need to get through it. Whether it's a counselor in your church or you go on a retreat or you read the Bible, you do something that gives you the support you need to get to the other end.

You also have to know what the end you want is. Do you want to be remarried? Do you just want to have a job and be a single mom? What is it? You need to reach out and ask for support; I think people really like to help other people. They're not always available because sometimes they're going through it themselves; but there's always someone with a helping hand. Often I think we let our pride get in the way. We let our stubbornness get in the way. We let our belief in how the world should be get in our way instead of dealing with how the world *is*. When we get that out of the way then we can start doing that which we need to do to get where we need to go.

Wright

If you could have a platform and tell our audience something you feel that would help or encourage them, what would you say?

Canfield

I'd say number one, believe in yourself, believe in your dreams, and trust your feelings. I think too many people are trained wrong when they're little kids. For instance, they're mad at their daddy and they're told, "You're not mad at your Daddy."

They say, "Gee, I thought I was."

Or you say, "That's going to hurt."

The doctor says, "No it's not." Then he or she gives you the shot and it hurts.

The doctor says, "See, that didn't hurt, did it?"

The result is you start not to trust yourself.

Or you ask your mom, "Are you upset?"

Your mom says, "No," but she really is. So you stop learning to trust your perception.

I tell the story over and over there are hundreds of people I've met who've come from upper class families where they make big incomes and the dad's a doctor, and the kid wants to be a mechanic and work in an auto shop because that's what he loves. The family says, "That's beneath us. You can't do that." So the kid ends up being an anesthesiologist killing three people because he's not paying attention. What he really wants to do is tinker with cars.

I tell people you've got to trust your own feelings—your own motivations, what turns you on, what you want to do, what makes you feel good—and quit worrying about what other people say, think, or want for you. Decide what you want for yourself and then do what you need to do to go about getting it. It takes work.

I always tell people that I read a book a week minimum and at the end of the year I've read fifty-two books. We're talking about professional books, books on self-help, finances, psychology, parenting, and so forth. At the end of ten years you've read 520 books. That puts me in the top one percent of people knowing stuff in this country. But most people are spending their time watching television.

W. Clement Stone told me when I went to work for him, "I want you to cut out one hour a day of television."

"Okay, what do I do with it?" I asked him.

He said, "Read."

He told me what kind of stuff to read. He said, "At the end of a year you'll have spent 365 hours reading. Divide that by a forty-hour work week and that's nine and half weeks of education every year."

I thought, "Wow! That's two months." It's like going back to summer school. As a result of that I have close to 8,000 books in my library.

The reason I'm on your show instead of someone else's is that people like me, Jim Rohn, Les Brown, and you read a lot. We listen to tapes and we go to those seminars. That's why we're the people with the information. I always say that your raise becomes effective when you do. You'll become more effective as you gain more skills, more insight, and more knowledge.

Wright

Jack, I have watched your career for over a decade and your accomplishments are just outstanding. But your humanitarian efforts are really what impress me. I think that you're doing great things, not only in California, but also all over the country.

Canfield

It's true. In addition to all of the work we do, we pick one to three charities. We've given away over six million dollars in the last eight years, along with our publisher who matches every penny we give away. We've planted over a million trees in Yosemite National Park. We've paid for hundreds of thousands of cataract operations in third world countries. We've contributed to the Red Cross, the Humane Society, and on it goes. It feels like a real blessing to be able to make that kind of a contribution in the world.

Wright

Today we have been talking with Jack Canfield, the founder and co-creator of the *Chicken Soup for the Soul* book series, which currently has thirty-five titles and I'll have to update this. It was fifty-three million. How many has it been now, Jack?

Canfield

We're almost up to seventy-eight million. We have a book coming out in just a couple of weeks called *Chicken Soup for the Soul of America*. It's all stories that grew out of 9/11—it's a real healing book for our nation. I would encourage your listeners to get themselves a copy and share it with their families.

Wright

I will stand in line to get one of those. Thank you so much for being with us today.

About Jack Canfield

Jack Canfield is one of America's leading experts on developing self esteem and peak performance. A dynamic and entertaining speaker, as well as a highly sought-after trainer, he has a wonderful ability to inform and inspire audiences toward developing their own human potential and personal effectiveness. Jack Canfield is most well known for the *Chicken Soup for the Soul* series, which he co-authored with Mark Victor Hansen, and for his audio programs about building high self-esteem. Jack is the founder of Self-Esteem Seminars, located in Santa Barbara, California, which trains entrepreneurs, educators, corporate leaders and employees how to accelerate the achievement of their personal and professional goals. Jack is also the founder of The Foundation for Self Esteem, located in Culver City, California, which provides self-esteem resources and training to social workers, welfare recipients and human resource professionals. Jack graduated from Harvard in 1966, received his M.E. degree at the university of Massachusetts in 1973, and an Honorary Doctorate from the University of Santa Monica. He has been a high school and university teacher, a workshop facilitator, a psychotherapist, and for the past thirty years, a leading authority in the area of self-esteem and personal development. As a result of his work with prisoners, welfare recipients, and inner-city youth, Jack was appointed by the state legislature to the California Task Force to Promote Self-Esteem and Personal and Social Responsibility. He also served on the board of trustees of the National Council for Self-Esteem.

Jack Canfield
P.O. Box 30880
Santa Barbara, CA 93130
Email: info4jack@jackcanfield.com

Chapter Three

DOUG DVORAK

Doug Dvorak

THE INTERVIEW

David Wright (Wright)

Today we are talking with Doug Dvorak. Doug Dvorak is a professional humorous speaker and creativity consultant who believes that "laughter is the software of the soul." Doug assists clients with improving their bottom line through the use of humor and creativity.

Doug's clients are characterized as Fortune 1000 companies, civic organizations and service providers. Doug is a certified creativity consultant, management consultant and corporate humorist. He holds a Bachelor of Arts degree in Business Administration and a Master of Business Administration in Marketing Management. Doug is also a graduate of the Player's Workshop of the Second City, one of the oldest and most prestigious improvisational comedy schools in the world. In addition, he is also active member of the National Speakers Association (NSA).

Doug, welcome to *Masters of Success*.

Doug Dvorak (Dvorak)

Thank you very much David, I'm glad to be here and may I say, you look fantastic. Are those paten leather?

Wright

Here we go! I am in for it aren't I? I'm surprised you didn't crack up with my mispronunciation of the word improvisational.

Dvorak

This obviously isn't "Masters of Speech." By the way, I love the humble, self-effacing title—*Masters of Success*. Let me guess, Gods of Greatness was already taken, most likely by a morning AA group in Des Moines?

Wright

Okay, okay, its time for the Jay Leno in me to come out even though I have no idea what to expect with this interview.

Dvorak

Gee, David, let's see, I am a *professional* speaker; and we are talking about my favorite subject—ME. This could go on for a couple of days; did you bring enough tape?

Wright

To start, perhaps you can share with us how you became a "Professional Humorist" Have you always been funny?

Dvorak

Excellent opening question Jay—I mean David—very professional and smoothly done. In other words, "It's time to talk about being funny!" Let's see, how did I start? Well, I started out as a poor child living in a doublewide. Wow, that is probably not a politically acceptable joke any longer. Actually I was a rich child living in a doublewide; well, not that rich. No, truthfully I was just always a pretty funny kid, with a good wit and a knack for finding the funny in all situations. Growing up I tended to rely on humor as a means to overcome my shyness and insecurities. I wasn't necessarily the "class clown"—more the Ed McMahon to the class clown, mostly working the smaller rooms—the lunchrooms, the math halls, that sort of thing.

As I went through college and began my professional life I informally continued to bring humor into my everyday life. Throughout my twenty-three-plus years as a professional sales person, my sales people and my managers repeatedly told me I had a good sense of humor and I was very creative, sometimes maybe a little too funny (but what did they know?).

In some ways I've always tried to use my humor and creativity as a way to manage my sales staff and build relationships with my clients. I simply have always believed that being funny helped me better connect with people.

Wright

How did you begin thinking about doing this professionally?

Dvorak

I guess when I started to consciously use my sense of humor as a means to my approach to business started for me back when I was a regional sales director for Boca Research, a manufacturer of data communications and IP telephony products based in Boca Raton, Florida.

Once while working for Boca I found myself tasked with developing an interesting and creative theme for our trade show booth at Comdex Canada, which, along with the Cured Meats Expo, is still one of the largest trade shows annually in Canada. It was there I had the good fortune to meet a very creative gentleman named Jim Ince. Jim was a professional entertainer who owned a special events company in Toronto. I was interviewing different creative talent trying to hit on a funny idea or theme when I was introduced to Jim and his company—Interactive Entertainment. We chatted for bit and together hit on an idea for a circus theme for the show. It would turn out to be one of the most successful themes of the entire Comdex show. Granted, our competition may have been a Jarts catching contest and a Molson keg give-away but still, we were funny and the show was a success. We even won a few awards for the themed circus booth concept, including the prestigious "Funniest Booth" prize that I made up and awarded our team.

So, through the course of the four-day trade show as Jim and I bantered back and forth doing some slap stick improvisation, we became instant friends and I am pleased to say remain so today. Jim has been a comedy mentor for me, actually helping me to further develop the character I use in my speeches—Dr. Earnest Carpediem. Together we also wrote the original keynote speech I still present to this day all over the world, "Mega Motivation with a Twist," with an obvious emphasis on the "twist."

It was also Jim who first suggested I seek some professional help. Now *that* is mentoring! Truthfully, he wasn't recommending I see a therapist—I was already seeing one of those—but rather that I should explore formal creativity and humor training and what better place then Chicago, the hometown for some of the best improvisation anywhere—The Second City Playhouse. He gave me the old, "if you can make it there kid, you can make it anywhere," speech. So I decided to make some calls. Through good fortune, talent, and persistence I landed a spot at the Players Workshop of the Second City, one of the oldest and most prestigious improvisational comedy schools in the world.

Wright

The Player's Workshop of the Second City in Chicago? Isn't that where Bill Murray, John Belushi, Dan Ackroyd, and Mike Myers studied improvisational comedy?

Dvorak

That's correct David. I entered their two-year program, Creative Expressions Through Improvisation—more properly titled, "Acting like an idiot—on cue"! What an experience. It essentially forced me to check the left hemisphere of my brain at the door once a week for two years. "Sorry Doug, no inhibitions allowed here today. I'm sorry, are you feeling a little self-conscious today? Do the next skit with your shirt off." It literally forced me to focus on the right side of my brain where humor, emotion, and creativity occur.

I have to say, the formal embracing of humor in my life blossomed from there. No, no David, there are five e's in hemisphere. So, as I advanced through the workshop and became more comfortable applying humor to real life situations I found my effectiveness as a sales professional was also improving as I was connecting with people on a more personal level. And the sales increased as well. Ah, the almighty dollar—there's nothing funny about greed, is there?

Wright

Can you tell us more about the influence that workshop had on your approach to humor and creativity?

Dvorak

Well, the Player's Workshop has such a tremendous history and reputation that it can be somewhat overwhelming for new students.

The two-year program begins with a basic introduction to improvisation and then advances quickly through a series of eight highly advanced improvisational classes. The class culminates with each student writing, directing, and producing their own *Saturday Night Live* type of skit for the main stage at Second City. It was there I first developed my alter ego, Dr. Earnest Carpediem, an obvious spoof on "seize the day."

When I first created the good doctor, I had no idea what he would become; he was simply this crazy motivational speaker I developed for a skit. The skit was very well received and the doctor became a regular at the workshop. The two-years were rewarding on many levels. The experience helped me to understand how the human mind processes humor and creativity; it also convinced me that humor, in its purest form, is actually risk and achieving humor is risk rewarded.

Wright

Will you share an example of how you applied what you learned in the workshop to the business world?

Dvorak

There is one story I like to share about taking a chance on humor. While I was still with Boca Research we had a booth at the Comdex computer show in Las Vegas, this one attracted more than 1.3 million people each year—a big show—our biggest show of the year. This time I was charged with coming up with the Chochki (Yiddish for Chochki) the giveaway—the trinket—companies use to help those who attend their booth remember their products.

So the show is approaching and I have nothing! Not a single decent idea; just mostly lame stuff like "the Boca spongy finger" or a Boca bouncing ball. I was nowhere. We are in Vegas, two days before the show and I'm out to dinner with my wife Cathy. After a magnificent all-you-can-eat buffet at The Mint, we were strolling downtown when somehow we discovered a novelty store—clearly divine intervention that I was able to find a novelty store in Vegas! So we wander in and I come across this propeller beanie. Boom! It hits me—technical people in the computer world are often referred to as "propeller heads." Did I really have something here or was this just a surefire way for me to offend 1.3 million technology professionals? I admit I was torn but I decided to take the risk and bet on the humor. So I ordered 25,000, had them embossed with "Boca Beanies" and shipped to Las Vegas within twenty-four hours to be handed out at our booth.

Wouldn't you know it—we ended up having the hottest give away at the show! The big guys—IBM and Microsoft—probably had huge budgets and teams of marketing gurus focus testing the "Micro-Frisbee," and here was Boca Research, on the second day of the show, being interviewed by CBS Evening News, *USA Today,* and *The Wall Street Journal,* all fascinated with the "Boca beanies."

I tell you that story not just because it makes me look great, but because I remember to this day that I had a critical decision to make and ultimately, I placed my bet on humor. I passionately believe that in all facets of life, one surefire way to break down walls and find commonality with people is through humor.

Wright

So when and how did your transformation from sales professional to a Professional Humorist begin?

Dvorak

The success at the Comdex show really got me going. More and more I began to count on humor, looking for ways to bring humor and creativity to my sales presentations, my client interactions, and subsequently into my speaking engagements. Soon my sales clients began asking me, "Can you help us out with our conference theme or can we pick your brain." You're kidding? Sure! You bet, how can I help? It was really getting exciting.

Wright

What convinced you that you could leverage your sales career into a speaking career?

Dvorak

As I mentioned David, sales has always been my profession. I was drawn to the excitement of carrying a sales quota and achieving the financial and personal rewards that come with accomplishment. Looking back, I now realize what I truly enjoyed doing was presenting during sales calls and conferences and infusing humor and creativity into my sales presentations. I guess I fell backwards into the old adage: find what you love to do and do it the rest of your life.

I loved the performance component of presenting to clients which in turn led to speaking opportunities for me with my sales clients. I also began networking within the speaking profession, joining an organization called Toastmasters International which is designed to help people of all professions become better speakers and communicators. I began attending more speaking seminars and conferences, getting introduced to some of the industry's best motivational speakers who are always willing to share their thoughts and ideas. It is a very nurturing profession filled with great people who helped me develop my passion for speaking. I feel like I am one of the luckiest men in the world to be doing what I am doing!

Wright

So what convinced you to make the leap permanently to being a Professional Humorist?

Dvorak

Well it was 1998; my sales job was on cruise control and I was doing well financially. I was also conducting outside speaking engagements about once a month so I was living the good life...or so I thought. Then that May, two life-changing events happened to me within days of each other that caused me to totally reevaluate who I was. As I share in my presentations in May, 1998, my dad died suddenly after a fall from a third story window and literally days later I was diagnosed with cancer—banner month in the Dvorak household, let me tell you.

Faced with both challenges I naturally became very reflective, as would anyone dealt with two life-altering curve balls. I could either have allowed those events to negatively impact my life or I could somehow find a way to move forward with a positive attitude. I admit, I struggled for weeks; but as I recall, I spent most of that time looking for ways to feel better, rather than going down a destructive path that could make things worse.

So, after weeks of soul searching, talking with my wife, my friends, family, and most importantly, myself, I reached a disturbing realization. Outside of my marriage, I had only one other true source of satisfaction and pleasure in my life and it was my speaking engagements. My job had become just that—a job. I was only really happy at my work when I was speaking, which was just not happening enough. I was conflicted and depressed. So, I made the very scary decision to quit my sales job. This was the time—the right time—for me to make the leap. I decided from then on I would do what I loved to do—speak professionally.

Wright

What led you to choose to speak professionally about humor, creativity, and motivation?

Dvorak

While I was working through the issues I was facing with my dad's death and then being diagnosed with cancer, I began reading the works of renowned author Dr. Norman Cousins. I owe so much of my recovery and my approach to humor to the works of Dr. Cousins and his writings on the healing power of laughter. Within his books, he describes how when you laugh—a good belly laugh—your body creates and emits endorphins. Now, these should not be confused with their close cousins, the Miami Endorphins. (Oh, come on Dave, I'm giving you pearls here.) Anyway, endorphins are the body's natural healing element.

Dr. Cousins noted that ten minutes of healthy laughter is equivalent to two hours of restful sleep. In his most famous book, written in the early '70s titled, *Anatomy of an Illness as Perceived by the Patient,* he documents his battle to overcome his life-threatening disease through the use of laughter. His doctors ostensibly gave him a death sentence—just a few months to live. He checked himself out of the hospital, went to a friend's cabin armed only with humorous materials—record albums, audiocassettes, and books that would make him laugh. All he did for six weeks was read, listen, and laugh. He came back after six weeks, marched right into his doctor's office for an exam, and walked out with a clean bill of health. That is a true story.

I read that book twice in one month trying to squeeze out every bit of hope. I sought out humor everywhere I could, maybe not to the degree Dr. Cousins did but with the same conviction. He was obviously a huge influence on me personally and helped me find my voice in humor and creativity. In fact, I found that if I indulged in a daily dose of humor, the following health benefits occurred:

- Laughter is a stress buster.
- It reduces the levels of stress hormones epinephrine and cortisol.
- Laughter strengthens the immune system.
- The immune system is important in maintaining good health by keeping infections, allergies, and cancers at bay.
- Laughter therapy helps to increase antibodies.
- Laughter is anti-ageing.

- It tones facial muscles and expressions.
- Laughter causes an increase in blood supply to the face, which is why some people look flushed. This nourishes the skin and makes it glow.
- People look younger and more fun when they laugh!
- Laughter is aerobic exercise.
- Laughter stimulates heart and blood circulation and is equivalent to any other standard aerobic exercise.
- One minute of laughter is equal to ten minutes on the rowing machine.
- The singular benefit almost everybody derives is a sense of well-being because more oxygen is taken in during laughter.
- Laughter is internal jogging.
- Laughter is a natural painkiller.
- Laughter increases the levels of endorphins—the body's natural painkillers.
- Laughter can control high blood pressure.
- Laughter can help dump depression and anxiety.
- Laughter makes you sleep better.
- Laughter improves lung capacity and oxygen levels in the blood.
- Laughter just makes you feel good.

Wright

How did you apply Dr. Cousins' philosophies on humor to your situation?

As is my nature, I took a very philosophical approach. I began to "investigate" the humor component of living; how other people who had personal and professional challenges stayed positive and how did humor play a role? I was convinced there would be a common thread there—humor somehow must have played a role in their recoveries. I began to devour books, audiocassettes, video programs, and anything I could get my hands on. I visited therapy centers and recovery units where I met with many who were battling life issues every day. The more I spoke with them, the clearer things became.

When they shared what was still positive in their lives, almost every one of their stories would involve humor. Here were people fighting to hold on to something, anything that was positive to keep them going and what they were able to find and grab hold of was humor.

Now, what really did it for me was the realization that I was, in fact, working through my grief in exactly the same way. What did I do when I was deeply depressed? I reached out for my source of humor—my speeches. Talk about an epiphany—I had used humor to recover. I soon began to feel better, and it was becoming easier to gain closure with my dad's death. My cancer treatments were continuing and I was growing stronger every day. Looking back, I am convinced I was actually receiving two forms of treatment—medical and humor and I thank God, because today I am cancer free, stronger, and a heck of lot wiser.

Wright

I'll share that with my wife; she is an eight-year cancer survivor.

Dvorak

God bless!

Wright

That means you're going to make it.

Dvorak

Yes, I am.

Wright

So you decided to throw all caution to the wind and begin a new career. What happened next?

Dvorak

It was after this experience that I created my own company committed to turn my *avocation* into my *vocation*. You like that don't you David? Make a note to remind me to make a note. With all humility, I named my company, Dvorak Marketing Group, created to help companies and business professionals achieve their business objectives through the use of humor and creativity. That's really how it all began David.

Wright

So tell me about how you began to approach clients and earned business for Dvorak Marketing Group?

Dvorak

My trade secrets David? Wait! Do I have more then one? My belief is that humor, creativity, and motivation—emotions and feelings that occur on the right side of our brain tend to be somewhat absent in today's political correct business environment, not to mention in our post 9/11 society. People are just not laughing enough. Since its inception, Dvorak Marketing Group has developed a number of assessment tools and selective exercises that take people through the creative process. We all have an IQ—an intelligence quotient and an EQ—an emotional quotient; but I believe we also all have an HQ—a humor quotient. I developed and designed a humor assessment that through a series of questions and phrases helps determine a person's humor quotient. We also provide our clients with exercises and suggestions all designed to develop the right side of their corporate brain.

Wright

So let's say I'm a prospective client. How do you explain how humor can boost employee moral and productivity?

Dvorak

I think that the vast majority of businesses today are too focused on the bottom line—got to make the numbers. It's all about making the numbers. But how do they get that done? The best companies do it with people. My position is that people really are the most productive when their personal goals are aligned with the goals of the organization. That's rather obvious but much is easier said then done.

Almost every company I meet with mentions one of their top corporate goals is to attract and retain quality people. Almost none of them have as part of their game plan a formal approach for injecting humor or creativity into the workplace. Now compare that to most employees' own personal mission statement, which typically includes "gaining more satisfaction out of their jobs" as one of *their* goals. See the disconnect? Making that connection is where I come in.

Case in point, take Herb Kelleher, the former CEO of Southwest Airlines. I have flown with Southwest on a number of occasions and I am a huge fan. I also have a close friend who is a captain for Southwest. She makes a very comfortable six-figure income flying and probably works only ten days a month. She loves her job. Who wouldn't? Once she told me a bit of internal scoop that made me think. Do you know what the most cherished reward a Southwest pilot can earn? It's the brown leather bomber jacket—a trophy respected industry-wide symbolizing they work for one of the finest company's in the world. That's creative, clever, motivational, and simple—I love it. And it doesn't stop there as anyone who has flown Southwest Airlines can attest. How about the fun the flight attendants are having? Certainly not your typical stodgy announcements at take-off from *this* crowd—they are encouraged to add humor and creativity, which helps them connect with their passengers. As an organization, top down, they have embraced a culture of creativity and humor which is why Southwest is continually recognized as one of the best companies to work for. They have made that connection. Unfortunately, I am not seeing enough of this from other CEOs in Corporate America today. My work is never done.

Wright

I have to ask, I know what a consultancy is but I am a little unclear—what is a humor creativity consultant?

Dvorak

It's funny because I am asked that constantly. This curious designation is bestowed upon only those individuals who attended and graduated from The Players Workshop at Second City. And, as I mentioned earlier, the actual program is called, Creative Expression Through Improvisation. The two-year program helps prepare its members to view life and work through a more creative and humorous set of lenses. It wasn't all just fun and games—the program really focused on the human psyche and how laughter and humor affects the brain.

I often boast to women that I have a doctorate in humor and creativity. It's a good thing I am married because even *that* line doesn't work for me. What I was finding as I began proactively seeking clients was that organizations of all types are in need of and are looking for ways to bring more humor and creativity into the personal and professional lives of their employees. I mean, look at the pressures people face today. Our lives are so complex with two-income households, raising kids, paying bills, saving for college, and caring for family members. I have taken to calling it the "sandwich generation." With so much coming at us each day that needs to be compressed?

What I was hearing back from companies who were hiring me was validating all of these concepts. The demand for my services remains strong because organizations are under tremendous pressures to meet their business needs. They are now recognizing the value of adding humor and creativity to the workplace.

Let me share an example. I'm currently working with an international airline on ways to infuse more humor and creativity into their rather staid senior management team. This group makes a wax museum look like a gymnastics competition. So we initially meet with their leadership team and discuss ways to customize the sessions to insure that it's fun and interactive while still meeting their specific needs.

We discussed a number of different types of exercises, even some that can take place outdoors, all designed to bring about different results. So we settled on a full day workshop built upon a scavenger hunt theme. Each attendee is asked to complete a humor and creativity assessment in advance of the workshop so going in they already have an idea of the areas where they need to improve. The assessment also gathers key personal preferences, such as an ability to communicate in a creative and humorous way, and what is the person's appetite for risk. This all becomes part of the session's key deliverable—our twenty-five-page individual profile—that we deliver at the end of the session. We call these "The Personality Owners' Manual." They are enlightening insights into each of the participant's psychological make-up that can hopefully benefit them well beyond the session. The Personality Owner's Manual focuses on helping the individual with:

- *Improved Communication* through a revealing exploration into the different ways team members send and receive information.
- *Reducing conflict,* tips on using humor and creativity to recognize and minimize unnecessary clashes between dissimilar personality types.
- *Strengthened Management Effectiveness* through increased awareness of the team, various human needs, and professional preferences.
- *Decreased Stress,* discovering ways to sidestep anxiety-generating and time-consuming interpersonal issues through the appropriate use of humor.

Ultimately, the team members learn to develop better relationships, improve morale, and create greater camaraderie through the healthy insights harvested during the workshop. And the results are typically so hilarious the teammates openly share their personal

Owner's Manual with others, further fostering the bond the session establishes.

So if you find yourself flying an airline in the near future and their personnel seem giddy as they run around hugging each other—we did something right. Or you just may be flying Southwest—one of the two.

Wright

I see you also do some writing as well.

Dvorak

Yes I do David. I have written two Harlequin Romance novels centered on a medieval Lord named Fronk who is allergic to tin.

Wright

Seriously?

Dvorak

Hello, professional humorist here! Actually, I have written two humorous books, at least I think they are funny; they are: *101 Twisted Mantra's For The New Millennium*™ and its highly anticipated follow-up, *101 Severely Twisted Mantras - For The New Age*™. I am also working on a number of humorous pamphlets I can leave behind to help my clients maintain the humor momentum. And you never know when I may write something else about Lord Fronk.

Wright

As you have worked to refine your role as a Professional Humorist, are there any professional people you consider your role models?

Dvorak

Well David, I think as I mentioned earlier, I not only have tremendous respect for Mr. Herb Kelleher as a superb business man, but also as leader with a great sense of humor. Early on while in graduate school, I read a business case about Southwest and the influence he has had on his organization. He stated that one of the driving forces behind their success was they created a culture that placed high value on the soft skills in his employees—energetic, fun-loving, and personable. So, right from the beginning Mr. Kelleher saw the value in recruiting and hiring a certain type of person who fit into their culture. This was at the beginning, way before their decade of rising stock and company value.

Another business leader, Victor Kiam, who is since deceased, once owned the NFL Patriots as well as Remington® shavers. He has written two books, *Going for it! How to Succeed as an Entrepreneur,* and *Live to Win: Achieving Success in Life and Business.* Within both books he shares story after story throughout his life of how he has taken risks and incorporated humor and creativity into his personal and professional life. He is especially proud of the time he brought a live chimpanzee on a sales call. Neither Mr. Kiam nor I am suggesting that any sales professional bring a chimp to a sales call—besides, any good salesperson calls ahead to check to see if the client already has one available. So to answer your question, I would say these two business leaders definitely influenced me and my career.

Wright

What about comedy professionals? Are there any you have looked to as role models or for inspiration?

Dvorak

Well initially, like many of my generation it was the masters: John Belushi, Dan Ackroyd, Gilda Radner, and Chevy Chase and their work on *Saturday Night Live.* I was transitioning from high school to collage just about the time they hit it big, so their styles and voices really hit the mark for me. I couldn't get enough of them—the show, their comedy albums, even seeing them come to Second City. Along with them, I have always found the impov work of Jonathan Winters and Robin Williams to be very free spirited—risk taking in its truest comic form. It's their risk taking, the high-wire act without a net that connects with the audience. Fans recognize they are out there taking a chance.

Another legend would be Don Rickles. The first time I had the privilege of seeing Don Rickles perform live was in Vegas in the early nineties. I was really fascinated at how much of Don Rickles' show is pure improv—just him playing off the audience—the brilliance, the simple brilliance. I stand in such awe of these artists who discovered their comic gifts then took the time, the energy, and the risks associated with turning those gifts into their own form of art.

Wright

I know he is not here, but if he was, what would Dr. Carpediem say are his motivational "do's and don'ts"?

Dvorak

Well, I know for a fact his biggest "do" is quite simply, "DO." We see so many books on how to stay motivated—people giving advice on what to do. People spend too much time learning about the how but don't spend enough time on the doing. Anyone who has seen Dr. Carpediem speak knows one of his favorite phrases is "Don't be known for what you say, be known for what you do."

Let's see, what are some other motivational "do's" from the good Doctor? Ah yes—taking motivational risks. This means get out of your mental comfort zones and push yourself to discover your humor and creativity. If you want to have more fun, and be more motivated, you have to take some risks, appropriate risks. Simple suggestions include: go to different places for dinner, or introduce yourself to people you see every day but may typically ignore—the people on your commuter trains, those working at the restaurant you visit regularly, and especially people you work with.

One of the doctor's favorite exercises with clients is the "happy fun guy." He challenges the audience to say, "Hi," to at least one stranger every day for one week. He bets a dinner that by Friday, everyone will have least one very funny experience. Most are leery but hey, think about the worst thing that can happen—you become known as the friendly guy? Come on! Shame on us for allowing our human nature to see risks where none exists. David, what is the opposite of risk?

Wright

Reward?

Dvorak

Good answer, but no. The true opposite of risk is regret. If you ask a person to share with you their biggest disappointments in life they will invariably tell you a story that includes regret. If I could pick just one message to come across to my audience, it would be that they walk away encouraged to take more risks in their personal and professional lives. Today will be gone forever, make it great and seize the day!

Wright

Doug I really appreciate your spending time with me here today. This has been enlightening and extremely enjoyable.

Dvorak

That's it? I didn't get to share the period of my professional life when I was a nude piano player working a health club lounge? Oh well, maybe next time. But sincerely David, thank you very much, it's been a privilege and a pleasure to share with you my philosophies on humor, motivation, and creativity.

Wright

Today we have been talking to Doug Dvorak, a professional humorous speaker and creativity consultant who believes that laughter is the software of the soul. Doug assists clients with improving their bottom line through the use of humor and creativity. I'm convinced he's right.

Doug thanks so much for being with us on *Masters of Success*.

Dvorak

Thank you David.

Doug Dvorak assists clients with productivity training, corporate creativity and humor workshops, and other aspects of sales and marketing management. Doug's clients are characterized as Fortune 1000 companies, small to medium businesses, civic organizations, service businesses, and individual investors and entrepreneurs. Doug Dvorak is a certified sales trainer, management consultant and corporate humorist. Doug holds a Bachelor of Arts degree in Business Administration and a Master of Business Administration in Marketing Management. But Doug's sense of humor is no less refined, as he is a graduate of the Player's Workshop of the Second City, one of the oldest and most prestigious improvisational comedy schools in the world. Doug has presented to over 50,000 people on four continents. Doug conducts personalized presentations and workshops. He speaks to management groups, business owners, and professional associations that appreciate his customized programs which never fail to bring smiles to people's faces. But regardless of Doug's comical presentations, he is a consummate business professional whose primary goal is client satisfaction. In addition, Doug is an active member of the National Speaker's Association® (NSA®).

Doug Dvorak

Phone: 847.359.6969

Mobile: 847.997.3454

Email: Doug@DougDvorak.com

www.DougDvorak.com

Chapter Four

JOHN CHRISTENSEN

JOHN CHRISTENSEN

THE INTERVIEW

David Wright (Wright)

Today we are talking with John Christensen. John's story begins in the shipping department at Chart House Learning where he began working as a teenager for his father, Ray. He worked his way to the top the old fashioned way, having to prove to his father and the company that he was a real filmmaker who could tell moving stories. Today Mr. Christensen guides Chart House as playground director, which is business talk for CEO, with an inspiring vision of an engaged workplace that can be developed through the *Fish Philosophy*. Chart House Learning is changing the way business is done worldwide. Like his dad before him, John created an eloquent language to transform lives. In 1997, he translated what happens daily at Seattle's world famous Pike Place Fish Market's culture into a vital global learning program called *Fish* and changed the entire business film industry. In the process, John also achieved his lifelong dream of how to turn workplaces into energetic, creative, and wholehearted endeavors with the four simple principles embodied in the *Fish Philosophy*.

John Christensen, welcome to *Masters of Success*.

John Christensen (Christensen)

Thank you, David. I appreciate that.

Wright

John, obviously, my first question is what are the four simple principles of *Fish Philosophy?*

Christensen

The four simple principles are play, make their day, be there, and choose your attitude.

Wright

Play? In other words we're supposed to play at work?

Christensen

Yes. Play is the basis of where creativity and innovation happens. And if you look back into your own life and see where you were most creative, it was in those moments of play and inspiration where you got lost in the moment. We call that play. Now if corporations are scared by that, think of it as lightheartedness. Think of it as taking your work seriously, but take yourself lightheartedly.

Wright

So tell us a little bit about what you do at Chart House Learning.

Christensen

We are kind of like cultural anthropologists. We study things that are out in the world, then we help put a language to it. For instance, that's what I saw at the fish market. I saw these fish mongers being totally engaged in their work and said, "Wait a minute! Wait a minute! There's something deeper going on than just play and all this craziness that I see on the shop floor." So we interpret that, then put a language around things, and help get that out into the business world. It's not only in the business world, schools are using it, too.

Wright

When you say "language," you're talking about terms that can be understood universally?

Christensen

Yes, absolutely. In *Fish,* it's ancient wisdom that's been resurfaced and brought to you in a new way and in an unlikely place—a fish market.

Wright

While preparing for this interview, I read that the first film in your series titled, *The Business Paradise* is the best selling film of all time. Is that true?

Christensen

Yes.

Wright

My goodness!

Christensen

Yes. That was first created in the '80s, with my father and a futurist. It's been translated in many, many languages. *Fish* is creeping up there, though. It's going to surpass *The Business Paradise* someday.

Wright

When you speak and train, how do you motivate people to create workplaces that are joyful and innovative, lighthearted and wholehearted?

Christensen

The interesting part of all this is when we tell them and they see the film or read the book, there's something that connects inside them that says either they had this in them or they were searching for this...this lightheartedness, this engagement of being at work and being engaged in what you do. We've made a film series with a poet named David White. David talks about being wholehearted. He has a friend, a monk friend, who said, "The way around burnout isn't necessarily burnout. It's being wholehearted in what you do." Now that's incredible. That says, if you come to work and you're totally engaged and enjoy what you are doing, the day goes by much quicker and you're going to be connected to it.

Wright

Do you find many CEOs, or especially upper management people, that are a little—

Christensen

Apprehensive of this?

Wright

Yes.

Christensen

Yes, there is. But the one's who embrace it and get it, stand back. Watch out for their organizations! For instance, the CEO of Aspen Ski Co., a ski company in Aspen, Colorado, who has embraced it said, "This is the pull; this is what we're going to be. This is the way we're going to service our employees. We're going to be engaged with what we do." They have 3500 seasonal employees. They teach them every year. They teach them the *Fish Philosophy* when the new group comes in, or even part of the old group comes in. They resurface this and say, "Remember, be engaged." And when they open that playing field and they give them the boundaries of saying, "Okay, safety is first in any business; here's the playing fields. Be safe. Don't do anything that's rude or crude." They saw things happening.

For example, like a guy—a young man—created his super hero called *Captain Iowa*. And he'd fly kids through the lift line up to the front and he'd help create an atmosphere in the lift line. When they're standing there for twenty-five minutes, that was engaging. They started karaoke in the waiting lines, and they do limbo in the waiting lines for the lifts. Now that created an atmosphere because, again, the CEO is saying, "Look, we have great snow and the same mountains as the other resorts. What separates us from the other people? What separates us from our other ski friends?" It was the way they engaged with customers.

That's the way, first and foremost, to have people engage in their work and be happy with where they are. I'm not just talking about making a "Pollyannaish" happy, happy workplace. I'm talking about people being engaged in what they do. Now if you have that and you create that kind of atmosphere, watch out! Your bottom line is going to go up. Your retention is going to go down.

Another thing that we find that's just really amazing is, when you step back and analyze it, we're in our places of work more than we are in our places of worship, more than we are in the great outdoors, and more than we are with our families. Now if we can't connect to that, be engaged and have a joyfulness to what we do, that's a sad statement saying, "Look at your life." Look at the hours you spend there, what are you giving it to? What are you spending your life's energy on? What are you giving, where are you giving your energy, your life energy too? Is this the place that you really want to be? Is this the place that's going to make you flourish?

Wright

What do you mean by "make their day?" Are these management theories that apply to employees, or are these employee theories that apply to customers?

Christensen

It includes absolutely everyone. It's employee-to-employee, it's employer-to-employee and it's employee to customer. It's the whole thing. I'm saying, if you come with that attitude, again, your life is about what you are giving to people. "Make their day" is just a new term of saying, be it, make people's day.

Serving others is when we really find joy. No matter if the CEO is talking to a vice-president or a president, or an employee is talking to a guest in a hotel, I'm saying make people's day! And it doesn't take much. It's really amazing the stories that we hear about the little nuances of what makes peoples' day. I mean, just being with a person—that moves into being there. What does "being there" mean? It means just being in the moment with a person. For example, if you're trying to talk to somebody in your office and you've got the phone ringing and a message on your cell phone, put all those distractions away. Let voicemail answer the phone, put the cell phone away, and be with the person. When you're in the presence of a person, they can feel it. Do I have time to share a story with you?

Wright

Sure.

Christensen

There was a policeman who was in the service area of a jail, the booking agent shall we say. The police department he worked for went through the *Fish Philosophy* teaching, and he got aware of being present and making people's day. The prison guard was totally in the moment with a shoplifter, who was being booked for shoplifting. He gave the person dignity and respect. The prisoner started to weep, saying, "I've never been treated this way in my life, much less I'm being booked for a crime I know I did." That's being present. That made that guy's day! That made that guy's life, maybe. Who knows?

Fish brings to the surface what people have in them. It gives them a way to say, "I can do this. I have permission. My organization has shown me the light of being "a day maker." Be private with people. When you're choosing your attitude, making people's day, and being present for people, guess what? The appropriate play comes out.

Wright

In reference to the third principle, choose your attitude, we're publishing a book for a man now about attitude. One of his favorite sayings is, "The difference between a good day and a bad day is your attitude."

Christensen

Absolutely. We all have magnificent stories about our lives. But if you look at people that have tragedies in some respect, and they come whistling in, what is that? How would we face some of these tragedies if they would happen to us? That is what we mean by choose your attitude.

Wright

John, I'd like to quote something you said referring to business. The quote is: "We need people who are passionate, committed, and free to live the organization's vision through their personal value." Would you explain what you were talking about?

Christensen

Yes. When you have an alignment with what you stand for as an individual and what the company, the organization, is standing for, step out of the way. Watch out! Watch the power that happens to that.

Wright

When you talk about businesses, you use words like "love" and "soul."

Christensen

Right.

Wright

Most people would think that spiritual values would not be appropriate in a business setting. Do companies accept your spiritual values as necessary ingredients to success?

Christensen

There's a whole new movement out there about spirituality. I want it to be clear. We're not talking religion. We're talking about the spirit and soul of people. And that brings the soul of a business alive. We made a film with Southwest Airlines. Southwest Airlines was founded on the following statement by Herb Kelleher and his two buddies: "We wanted to create a workplace based on love rather than fear." Now, if Southwest Airlines with 33,000 employees is based on love and is doing incredibly well in the airline industry, is that not a valuable statement to everybody in business?

Wright

Is there anything or anyone in your life that has made a difference for you and helped you to become a better person?

Christensen

I have a lot of mentors in my life. My parents have been incredible mentors. My mom was a social worker and a very incredible people woman, and my dad was an artist. And when you combine those two, they've been wonderful mentors for me. I've also had the blessings of having Ken Blanchard as a mentor and Spencer Johnson. So I've had great mentors in that respect, too.

Wright

I was talking to Jim Cathcart the other day. I told him that one of my mentors had no knowledge of his being a mentor, and that was Bill Gove from Florida who I have been listening to his talks and tapes and reading his books for probably forty years.

What do you think makes up a mentor? In other words, are there characteristics that mentors seem to have in common?

Christensen

I believe they're different for everybody. I mean everybody finds a different mentor. I think some of the beautiful mentorships happen when a person takes you under their wing.

Another inspiration for me is Norman Vincent Peale. Okay, he's got religion in there, but his being was a mentorship for me. His presence, the way he spoke so eloquently and so much passion, that's what mentored me. You can get inspired by many different things. If a tape or a book inspires you and becomes your mentor, fabulous. When it opens you up to the possibilities in your life, be it a book, a mentor, a tape, a film, they are all wonderful aspects of opening you up to possibilities.

Wright

I remember when I was in Seattle a few years ago and saw the people working in the company that you wrote about, I remember two feelings. One is a feeling that this would be a nice place to buy something. But the biggest feeling was these guys are really happy and fun. And they've got a tough job too. That's not one of your bank president's type jobs.

Christensen

No. Hey, they don't work in air conditioning in the summer and heating in the winter. They work with dead fish, ice and cold cement floors. I've wiped out there many a time. It's just showing you the possibilities that if they can do it with their hands in dead fish, cold ice, and twelve-hour days, that's what's so powerful about it. That's why we call it the *Fish Philosophy*. It's based on the fact that if the fish market can do it, you can do it. But the philosophy is ancient wisdom but it's coming alive on a fish market. And if a fish market can do it, we all can do it.

Wright

We've talked about three out of four of the principles; the last one I'd like to ask you about is the principle "be there." Do you mean come to work on time and be there? Or be there for people?

Christensen

Be there for people. I mean absolutely be in the moment. Like I was saying, when you're with somebody, put the other things down. I catch myself so many times sitting at my desk when people come in, and I'm reading something, or half with them or not. You have to take that moment and put what you're doing down and be there for them. Another good little exercise to do is when the phone rings, take a moment before you pick it up and just pause. Think about what you're going to do on the phone. It doesn't matter if it's a sales person or whatever, just remember to be there in the moment when you're on the phone with a person. It's an interesting little exercise of being present.

Wright

Most people are fascinated with these new television programs about being a survivor. What has been the greatest comeback you have made from adversity in your career or in your life?

Christensen

Wow! The biggest adversity? Well, there are two. We went through a stint with a company where some people tried to take over our business, and I made it through that. But one of the things was living up to my mentor—my father—and having knowing in my heart and my gut that I had the capacity to leave the company and to be a great filmmaker like my father. And I don't mean great in a cocky way. I'm saying bringing what we bring to the table of documentaries. Showing the world what possibilities are. That's what I mean by great. That was a high. That was a hurdle to work through.

Wright

When I was researching for this interview, I noticed on your website they also referred to Joel Barker, the futurist who helped your father.

Christensen

Futurist, correct.

Wright

And so your father started making what? Documentary films?

Christensen

Yes. He started off in advertising just when television was getting started in the late '50s. He happened to be in love with the documentary approach. He pursued the documentarian lifestyle and would go off and make films. What he brought to the table was this uniqueness, this anthropological aspect into looking at things, studying it, and saying, "What can we do to show that?" For instance, when his career started off in Omaha, Nebraska, he made a film about the city of Omaha. But through the whole film, you didn't know where you were until the end of the film, *Come See Our City, Omaha*. But it showed you who the people were, what the organizations were like in Omaha, and you'd like to come and live here and build your business here. So he brought that approach to it. Let's study it. Let's bring it. Let's show people what it's about instead of telling them, Again, that's what happened with the paradigm idea. Let's look at a paradigm. Let's look at it all these different ways. If it doesn't get you this way, look at it this way. Look at it this way. If this story doesn't connect with you, look at it this way. Ah, and then you can relate to that.

Wright

The free-wheeling workplace of the 1990s is long gone. Companies are cutting perks. Employees are reverting from casual attire to business wear. How can employees really play at work when the reins are being pulled back so tightly?

Christensen

Well, that's our point. The reigns shouldn't be pulled back so tightly. Ken Blanchard calls it the tight underwear syndrome. We need to get rid of that. We need to free people up because when you're free is when creativity and innovation happens. I don't know where the quote comes from, but it was said, "If works were plays, Silicon Valley would not have been created." Because it would out the play. Two guys in their garage, I mean how many guys were in their garage playing, tinkering around, right? Hewlett Packard, Apple, I mean how many more can we list? They were playing!

See, it's the playfulness in which they react to each other and react to customers at the fish market. You can see what they're doing and make your own style. It opens you up to say, "What can *we* do that is about playfulness?"

Wright

I've heard about the impact that *Fish* is having on corporate America. Has it been used outside the business world?

Wright

Schools are one of our biggest clientele. It's amazing. We are now creating a curriculum for schools. We're working on creating how to bring this in. If you could talk about being present to what you are doing and making people's day to elementary students, imagine what possibilities lie in the future for that!

Wright

Are you having more success getting it into the private schools or public schools?

Christensen

Public schools are embracing it. First and foremost, what's happening is that the administration and the teachers are being brought into this, talking about how they can engage with their work. Again, you said the budget crunches and the tightening of the ropes, and with all that, how are we going to? It goes back to saying, "What kind of organization can we be that is going to help people be engaged in what we're here for?"

We have a roofing company that used this that turned their entire company around into roofing, and now they're a world famous roofing company. They get roofing jobs in different places in the world. They just showed up in a different way. They were being something different.

Now, back to education. If you are being present in the classroom for your kids as a participant, not even as customer you're saying, "They're the 'customers,' I have to serve them." They're there to teach you as much as you are there to teach them. My goodness! That was my first love. I wanted to be a teacher saying, "What can you bring to the table?"

John Keating in the film *Dead Poets Society* is the kind of teacher we need—people engaged in the minds of our youth saying, "How do I get to them? How do I reach them? How am I there with them? What do I do to make their day?" We're actually working on the concept of saying the four principles of *Fish* are the rules of the classroom. What am I doing today to play, to be playful? This works both ways. This is teacher and student, partner-to-partner. What are we doing to make the classroom fun? What are we doing to make each other's day? How am I being there for you? How are you being there for me? How are you being there for your other your peers? And first and foremost, how are you choosing to come to school? How are you choosing to be today?

Wright

Very interesting. Boy, this has been a fast, fast thirty minutes, and I really do appreciate your being a guest today. I really appreciate you taking the time.

Today we have been talking with John Christensen whose story began as he said working with his father as a great role model. You've heard the intelligent statements and how the *Fish Philosophy* can literally change you and your company's future, as it's changing some in America.

So, let me ask you before we leave, I'd like to shamelessly advertise the book. I think everyone should read it. I know you're making good at Amazon.com. Can people get it direct from you or can they find out more on your website? If you'll give us that information, I would appreciate it.

Christensen

Absolutely. It is available at www.charthouse.com. Inside of charthouse you can go to fishphilosophy.com, which is a whole website with all the fish information. You can purchase all sorts of our films including our ancillary products, our fishing gear, and you can purchase the books. Now there are two books on the market, David. There's *First Fish!* and our second one that came out in April called *Fish Tales*.

Wright

I hope our readers and our listeners will rush to the website and get this book. I've got *Fish Tales*. I'm going to get the first one.

Christensen

Thank you, David. Thank you so much. I really appreciate your time.

About John Christensen

John Christensen's story begins in the shipping department at ChartHouse Learning where he began working as a teenager for his father, Ray. He worked his way to the top the old-fashioned way, proving to his father—and the company—that he was a real filmmaker who could tell moving stories. Today Christensen guides ChartHouse as "Playground Director" (CEO in business-speak) with an inspiring vision of an engaged workplace that can be developed through the FISH! Philosophy. The rest of the story is that ChartHouse Learning is changing the way business is done worldwide. "The ChartHouse vision is an invitation to people to become fully immersed in their lives, using these four seemingly simplistic ideas," he says. "In many ways the FISH! Philosophy is really ancient wisdom for modern times, a lifestyle choice to engage in life-long learning and self-improvement. The products we offer are really learning tools, from some of the best mentors one could have—real-life experiences that ultimately speak to the human spirit." Today John speaks to vastly different organizations about his journey—the serendipitous discovery of the fish market—and how that simple FISH! Philosophy he and his team poetically articulated on film four years ago can dramatically change the stories of companies and individuals.

John Christensen
www.charthouse.com
www.fishphilopophy.com

Quick Order Form

Telephone Orders: Call 847-359-6969
Have your credit card ready.

Email Orders: doug@dougdvorak.com

Postal Orders: DMG, Inc.
Doug Dvorak
50 South Greeley, #413
Palatine, IL 60067, USA
Telephone: 847-359-6969

Please send the following books. I understand that I may return any of them
for a full refund—for any reason, no questions asked.

_____
_____
_____
_____

Please send more FREE information on:

☐ Other Books   ☐ Speaking/Seminars   ☐ Consulting

Name:
Address: _____
City: _____ State: _____ Zip: _____
Telephone
Email address: _____

Sales tax: Please add 9.75% for products shipped to Illinois addresses.

Shipping by air

US: $5.00 for first book and $2.00 for each additional product.

International: $9.00 for first book; $5.00 for each additional product (estimate).

Quick Order Form

Telephone Orders: Call 847-359-6969
Have your credit card ready.

Email Orders: doug@dougdvorak.com

Postal Orders: DMG, Inc.
Doug Dvorak
50 South Greeley, #413
Palatine, IL 60067, USA
Telephone: 847-359-6969

Please send the following books. I understand that I may return any of them
for a full refund—for any reason, no questions asked.

_____
_____
_____

Please send more FREE information on:

☐ Other Books   ☐ Speaking/Seminars   ☐ Consulting

Name: _____

Address: _____

City: _____ State: _____ Zip: _____

Telephone _____

Email address: _____

Sales tax: Please add 9.75% for products shipped to Illinois addresses.

Shipping by air

US: $5.00 for first book and $2.00 for each additional product.

International: $9.00 for first book; $5.00 for each additional product (estimate).

Made in the USA
Middletown, DE
25 October 2021